Biggest, Baddest Books for Boys

BIGGEST, BADDEST BOOK OF WARRIORS

ANDERS HANSON & ELISSA MANN

Consulting Editor, Diane Craig, M.A./Reading Specialist

A Division of ABDO

ABDO
Publishing Company

Visit us at www.abdopublishing.com

Published by ABDO Publishing Company, a division of ABDO, P.O. Box 398166,
Minneapolis, Minnesota 55439. Copyright © 2013 by Abdo Consulting Group, Inc.
International copyrights reserved in all countries. No part of this book may be
reproduced in any form without written permission from the publisher. Super
SandCastle™ is a trademark and logo of ABDO Publishing Company.

Printed in the United States of America, North Mankato, Minnesota
062012
092012

♻ PRINTED ON RECYCLED PAPER

Editor: Liz Salzmann
Content Developer: Nancy Tuminelly
Cover and Interior Design and Production: Anders Hanson, Mighty Media, Inc.
Illustration Credits: Shutterstock

Library of Congress Cataloging-in-Publication Data

Hanson, Anders, 1980-
Biggest, baddest book of warriors / Anders Hanson and Elissa Mann.
   p. cm. -- (Biggest, baddest books for boys)
Audience: Ages 4-10.
ISBN 978-1-61783-409-7 (alk. paper)
1. Soldiers--Juvenile literature. 2. Military history--Juvenile literature. I. Mann,
Elissa, 1990- II. Title.
U750.H37 2013
355.33'--dc23

                                                                    2011050910

Super SandCastle™ books are created by a team of professional educators, reading specialists, and
content developers around five essential components—phonemic awareness, phonics, vocabulary, text
comprehension, and fluency—to assist young readers as they develop reading skills and strategies and
increase their general knowledge. All books are written, reviewed, and leveled for guided reading, early
reading intervention, and Accelerated Reader® programs for use in shared, guided, and independent reading
and writing activities to support a balanced approach to literacy instruction.

CONTENTS

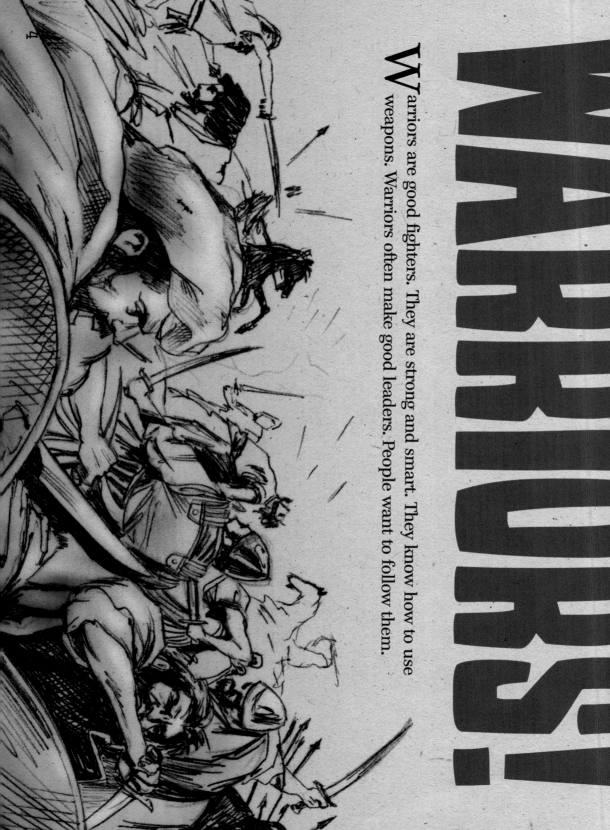

WARRIORS!

Warriors are good fighters. They are strong and smart. They know how to use weapons. Warriors often make good leaders. People want to follow them.

BRAVERY

Warriors are very brave. They know that the dangers they face are real. But they face them anyway! This makes the people around them feel brave too.

HONOR

Honor is an important part of being a warrior. Warriors don't just want to kill people. They fight for causes they believe in.

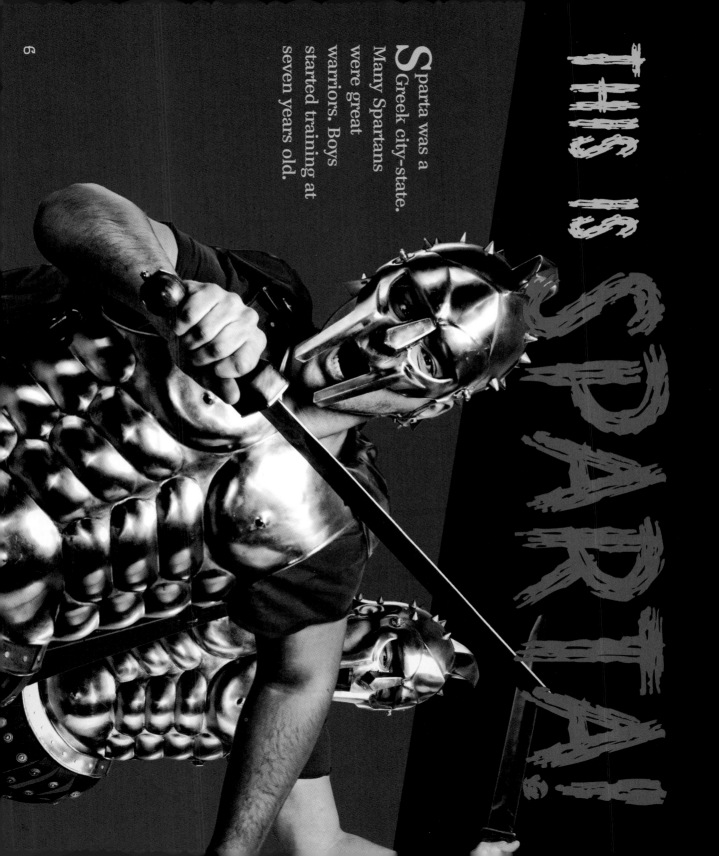

Sparta was a Greek city-state. Many Spartans were great warriors. Boys started training at seven years old.

THIS IS SPARTA!

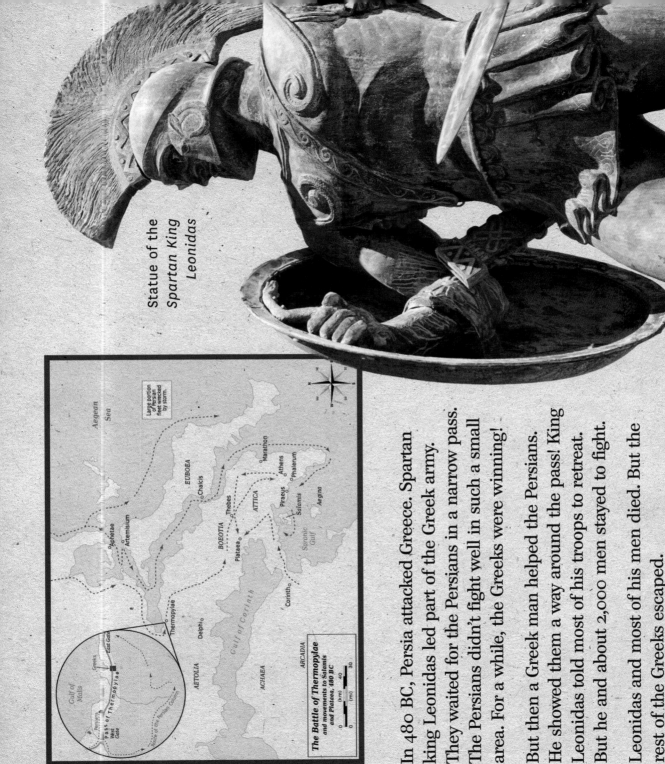

Statue of the
Spartan King
Leonidas

The Battle of Thermopylae
and movements to Salamis
and Plataea, 480 BC

Large portion
of Persian
fleet wrecked
by storm.

Aegean
Sea

EUBOEA

Aphetae

Artemisium

Chalcis

Thermopylae

Delphi

BOEOTIA

Plataea

Thebes

Marathon

Athens

ATTICA

Piraeus

Phalerum

Saronic
Gulf

Salamis

Aegina

AETOLIA

Gulf of Corinth

Corinth

ACHAEA

ARCADIA

Gulf
of Melis

Pass of Thermopylae

East Gate

Greeks

West
Gate

Route of the Persian Column

In 480 BC, Persia attacked Greece. Spartan
king Leonidas led part of the Greek army.
They waited for the Persians in a narrow pass.
The Persians didn't fight well in such a small
area. For a while, the Greeks were winning!

But then a Greek man helped the Persians.
He showed them a way around the pass! King
Leonidas told most of his troops to retreat.
But he and about 2,000 men stayed to fight.

Leonidas and most of his men died. But the
rest of the Greeks escaped.

HANNIBAL

Hannibal Barca was one of the greatest generals in history. He led a large army to attack Rome.

Hannibal's army
crossing the Alps

Hannibal's army
included more than
70,000 men. He also
had 37 war elephants!

Hannibal and his army
won many battles
against the Romans. He
ruled parts of northern
Italy. But he never
conquered Rome.

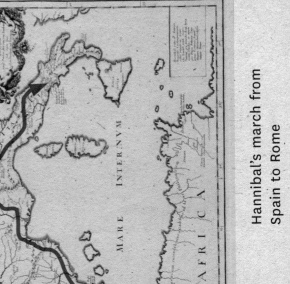

Hannibal's march from
Spain to Rome

VIKING WARRIORS

Viking lands (in red) in the eighth century

The Vikings were warriors of the sea. They lived hundreds of years ago. They came from northern Europe.

MASTERS OF THE HIGH SEAS

Vikings were great sailors. They built boats called longships. They were very fast! They could make long trips across the ocean.

DISCOVERY OF NORTH AMERICA

Leif Ericson was the first European in North America. He landed in Canada about 1,000 years ago.

MYTH BUSTER

Many people think Viking hats had horns. But that's not true! Most of them did not have horns.

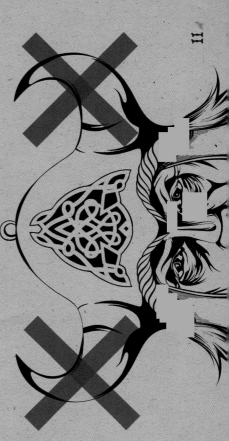

Medieval Knights

Knights were great warriors. They lived during the Middle Ages.

Jousting was a favorite sport of knights.

CAVALRY

Knights rode horses into battle. The horses had armor too!

ARMS AND ARMOR

Knights wore heavy suits of armor. They also used shields. Their weapons were swords and lances.

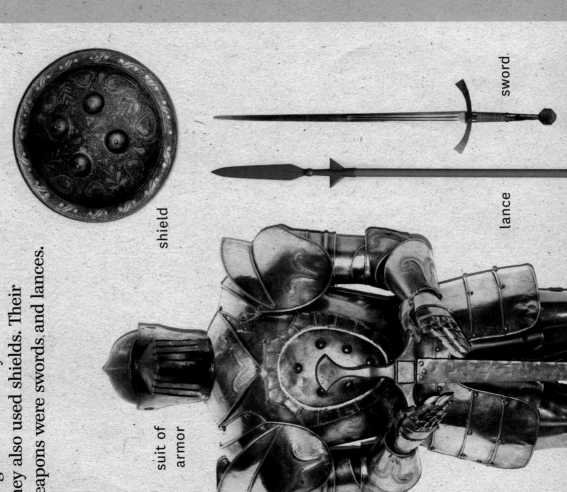

shield

sword

lance

suit of armor

Genghis Khan

and the Mongols

No warrior conquered as much land as Genghis Khan. He **united** all of Mongolia. Then he went on to conquer much of Asia and Eastern Europe.

The Mongol Empire was one of the largest ever.

HORSE AND BOW

The Mongols rode horses into battle. This allowed them to attack and retreat quickly.

The Mongols were also excellent archers. Their bows were small. They were easy to use on horseback.

ALEXANDER "THE GREAT"

Alexander was only 20 when he was crowned king of Macedonia. But he was ready to lead his people. He learned from a great teacher named Aristotle.

Alexander was a brilliant leader. He never lost a battle!

Alexander and his teacher, Aristotle.

Alexander's empire at the time of his death

JOAN OF ARC

Joan of Arc was born in France around 1412. France was at war with England. The French were losing.

Joan started hearing voices when she was 12. She saw visions too. They told her to take her country back from the English!

At first people thought she was crazy. Then she led the French army in many successful attacks on the English. The French started winning. She saved her country!

Joan of Arc was captured in 1430. She died in 1431. Today, Joan of Arc is a French national hero.

william wallace

Guardian of Scotland

England attacked Scotland in 1296. William Wallace wanted to defend his country. So he formed his own army. It was a small, ragged army.

"Freedom is best, I tell thee true, of all things to be won."

—William Wallace

"We come here with no peaceful intent, but ready for battle, determined to avenge our wrongs and set our country free."

—William Wallace, before the Battle of Stirling Bridge (September 11, 1297)

The Wallace Monument is in Stirling, Scotland. The tower overlooks the Stirling Bridge battlefield.

Battle of Stirling Bridge

In 1297, Wallace's small army attacked a huge English army as they crossed Stirling Bridge. About 5,000 English soldiers were trapped. Wallace won the battle. The rest of the English went back to England.

Shield at the Wallace Monument

"MAD JACK" CHURCHILL

M ad Jack Churchill was a British Commando in WWII. He was given a gun. But he wanted to bring his sword and a longbow too! He once started a battle by shooting a German officer with his bow.

Mad Jack loved to play the bagpipes. He often played while marching into battle. The Germans captured Mad Jack twice. But he escaped both times!

"Mad Jack" with his sword

"Mad Jack" looking down the barrel of a huge gun

"ANY OFFICIER WHO GOES INTO ACTION WITHOUT HIS SWORD IS IMPROPERLY DRESSED."

—"Mad Jack" Churchill

WHAT DO YOU KNOW ABOUT WARRIORS?

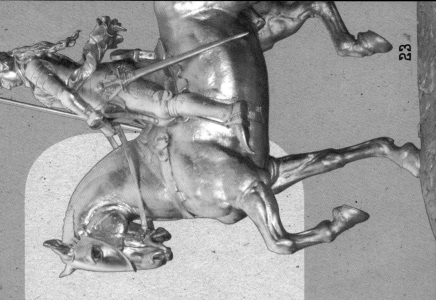

1. IT'S IMPORTANT FOR WARRIORS TO BE HONORABLE. **TRUE OR FALSE?**

2. HANNIBAL NEVER CONQUERED ROME. **TRUE OR FALSE?**

3. THE VIKINGS WERE FROM AUSTRALIA. **TRUE OR FALSE?**

4. THE SAMURAI DID NOT LIVE BY RULES. **TRUE OR FALSE?**

ANSWERS: 1) TRUE 2) TRUE 3) FALSE 4) FALSE

GLOSSARY

ARCHER – a person who uses a bow to shoot arrows.

CULTURE – the ideas, traditions, art, and behaviors of a group of people.

DEFEND – to protect from harm or attack.

JOUST – a contest in which two knights ride horses toward each other and use lances to try to knock each other down.

MIDDLE AGES – the period of history in Europe from about AD 500 to about AD 1500.

UNITE – to join two or more things together.